What others are say
Courier Air Trave

"If you're looking for a bottoı ̣ ̣ ̣ ̣ ̣ , ̣ ̣ ̣ ̣ ̣ ̣ ̣ ̣ ̣ ̣ ̣ ̣ ̣ ̣ ̣ er
trips can't be beat. For valuable information, check out
the *Courier Air Travel Handbook* by Mark Field."
— *Cosmopolitan Magazine*

"Enterprising travelers should consider flying as a
courier. Check out Mark Field's Courier *Handbook*."
— *Let's Go Travel Guides*

"This just might be one of the best book purchases you
ever make."
— *Bethany, OK Tribune*

"Air couriers can fly free or at substantially reduced
cost. The *Courier Air Travel Handbook* by Mark I. Field
tells how."
— *Ft. Myers News-Press*

"Fly to Worldwide Destinations for as little as $99
roundtrip, or even free."
— *Transitions Abroad Magazine*

"This little-known method of travel is accessible to
virtually anyone with this handy book."
— *Greensboro, NC News & Record*

"This book explains the cheapest way to fly..."
— *Arizona Daily Star*

"Save BIG on airfare! Don't waste your money on expensive airfare... Fly courier."
— *Miami Entertainment News*

I travel not to go anywhere, but to go. I travel for travel's sake. The great affair is to move.

–Robert Louis Stevenson
1850–1894

Travel, in the younger sort, is a part of education; in the elder, a part of experience.

–Francis Bacon
1561–1626

Travel is one way of lengthening life, at least in appearance.

–Benjamin Franklin
1706–1790

Il faut être toujours botté et prêt à partir.
One should always have one's boots on and be ready to leave.

–Michel de Montaigne
1533—1592

COURIER

AIR TRAVEL

HANDBOOK

Learn How to Travel For Next to
Nothing to Cities Around the World

By

Mark I. Field

Third Edition

Thunderbird Press
5930-10 W. Greenway Road
Suite 112B
Glendale, Arizona 85306

ISBN: 0-9630613-0-5

Printed in the United States of America

First Printing: July 1990
Second Printing: August 1991–2nd edition–Completely revised
Third Printing: November 1991
Fourth Printing: December 1991
Fifth Printing: February 1992
Sixth Printing: May 1992–3rd edition–Completely revised

Published by:
Thunderbird Press
5930-10 W. Greenway Road
Suite 112B
Glendale, Arizona 85306

Distributed to the U.S. Book Trade by PDS (800) 345-0096.
Retail Sales in the U.K. by John Walker, 160 Cromwell Road, London SW5 0TL, England, 071-373-3083

Book design by Carla Hewitt
Illustrations by Cindy Lacotta and Carla Hewitt
Book cover design by Bob Silverman
Cover photos courtesy of Andy M. Clarke and Kirsten C. Weiss

About the Author

Mark I. Field is an avid world traveler. He is originally from New York City and now makes his home in Arizona. Prior to attending college, he spent eight years in the United States Navy serving on submarines. He is a graduate of the University of Arizona with a degree in Business Economics and is presently attending the American Graduate School of International Management where he will earn a Master's Degree in International Management with an emphasis in international marketing.

Mark was inspired to write this book because during his travels he encountered so many people who knew little or nothing about courier travel. He felt more people would have the opportunity to travel if they only knew about this concept. "The ability to travel should not be decided by one's financial position," he asserts. On one of his trips Mark backpacked throughout Europe on an extremely limited budget... and had the time of his life. Besides travel, Mark also enjoys basketball, scuba diving and skydiving.

DEDICATION

This book is dedicated to my mother, **Betty Lou Field**, who inspired in me a desire to travel and see the world.

ACKNOWLEDGMENTS

The author wishes to thank the following people:

- Lisa A. LaVoie for being the woman behind my motivation.

- Mindy Bingham
- James L. Booth, Jr.
- Robin W. Booth
- Daniel F. Brogan
- Bosworth Dewey
- Craig Edwards
- Nicky Gonzalez
- Sarah D. Hanson
- Carla Hewitt
- Jeffrey J. Leslie
- Xiaoe Liu
- Jeffrey I. Miller, M.D.
- Rachel A. Miller

- Martha Moss
- Ralph Moss, Ph.D.
- Dan Poynter
- Gillian Rice, Ph.D.
- Eric D. Sachs, J.D.
- Marjorie H. Sachs, J.D.
- Andy Shapira
- Jill A. Smith
- Mark Weinstein, J.D.
- Kirsten C. Weiss

A Note on
Prices and Destinations

The courier industry, like the travel industry, changes constantly. Every effort has been made to provide the reader with accurate information, and all the information in this book is based on the best information available at the time of publication.

Prices, destinations, phone numbers and other pertinent information in this book are subject to change. It is important to realize that courier companies may go out of business, change their policies concerning onboard couriers, or simply change their phone numbers.

If you come across any new information, please write to me in care of the publisher. If I include it in the next edition of this book, I will acknowledge your contribution and send you a free copy of the book.

Mark I. Field

Questions and Answers About Courier Travel

Q: Who can travel as a courier?

A. Anyone who is over the age of 18 and has a valid passport. You need not be a citizen of the country in which the courier flights orginate. If you are a traveler, student, teacher, retiree, businessperson, adventurer, or just interested in saving money, you are an ideal candidate for courier travel.

Q: Will I have to transport anything illegal?

A: Absolutely not. The courier industry is a respectable industry. The types of items that you will transport include documents, files, boxes, computer disks, contracts, and so on. You will NOT have to load the material. The courier company takes care of that on both ends.

Q: What are the benefits of courier travel?

A: The money you save. As a courier, you will only pay a small percentage of the cost of the plane ticket.

Q: What are the drawbacks of courier travel?

A: You usually will only be allowed to take carry-on bags with you. The courier company transports items in place of your luggage.

Q: Can I pay the airline money to take an extra bag?

A: Most airlines will allow you to take extra baggage if you pay an additional baggage charge, but in most cases it is not worth the extra money. If you *must* take your wardrobe, then courier travel may not be for you. In that case, give this book to a friend!

TABLE OF CONTENTS

Part I

ABOUT COURIER TRAVEL

W hat is a courier? A courier is a person who delivers something for someone. An air courier is an individual, such as yourself, who acts as the agent simply by occupying a seat on the plane, and therefore, permits the courier company to transport packages by air. Federal Express, UPS, and Emery are examples of air courier companies, and there are literally hundreds of such companies in the United States, though most of them are lesser known than Federal Express, UPS, and Emery.

Air courier companies often solicit people to act as air couriers. By acting as an air courier you allow the company to make its deliveries by giving up the right to check in luggage in exchange for a cheaper airfare. Courier travel is one of the cheapest and simplest ways to travel around the world. It is ideal for students, senior citizens, vacationers and even business travelers.

Travel as an air courier is safe. You will not be transporting anything illegal; this is a very respectable industry. These companies are insured and bonded, and the courier company will not attempt to ship anything questionable. The items that you will transport include documents, books, blueprints, supplies, equipment, checks, and so on. It is important to know that the courier company will turn the material over to the airline, and they will retrieve the material upon completion of the flight. You, the courier, will never see or touch the actual shipment.

Every year thousands of people travel around the world as couriers. This book will tell you step-by-step how to become an air courier. You can begin today to travel to many exciting cities around the world for a fraction of the normal cost of coach fares.

Why Are Couriers Used?

Years ago there were only a few companies that could (or would) transport material overseas. Today that has changed. The world has become closer, more accessible. More and more companies are relying on overseas business. In fact, many of the leading industries for the 1990's involve international travel—international lawyers, import/export traders and international businesses. European and Asian manufacturers and markets have become of vital importance to the continuing growth of the United States economy. As more companies expand into this market, the greater the necessity for courier companies and agents called couriers.

The economics behind the courier industry are quite simple. The FAA requires that all overseas flights must have a passenger for the checked luggage. This policy is not the same for domestic flights, although there are some domestic courier flights available.

A courier company will purchase a round trip ticket in advance to an overseas destination. This ticket might cost the company $600. They, in turn, take orders to ship material for that day. A courier company will charge about $50 to deliver a small package overseas; large, heavy, or expensive items can be delivered for an even higher price. The courier company could generate up to $5,000 in revenue per flight.

The company then turns around and sells you their $600 round trip ticket for as low as $99. According to this example, the company would bring in roughly $4,500 in profit. This is the reason why they can afford to sell you the plane ticket so cheaply.

The courier company offers the plane ticket to the general public at a discounted price in order to recoup some of their money. If the courier company cannot sell the ticket, or if they have a cancellation, then the ticket may be given away for free. This happens fairly often, as it is better for the company to take a loss on the $600 ticket than to send an employee who would have to be paid for his time as well as his expenses. Simply put, it is in the best interest of the courier company to offer the ticket for sale to the general public.

Traveling as a courier is similar to traveling as a full-paying passenger—the only difference is the access to the information in this book. Couriers are sent on major airlines including United, TWA, American, British Airways, Northwest and Singapore Airlines. As an air courier, you will be treated like any other passenger. In fact, nobody will know that you are an air courier unless you tell them. Additionally, you will usually get to keep the frequent flyer mileage. The person next to you might be paying $500 more for their seat. So you see, there is little inconvenience compared to the tremendous savings.

Worldwide Destinations

The first step in traveling as an air courier is to determine where you want to visit. Remember that not all cities are serviced by all the courier companies. For example, you might use one company to travel to Sydney and another to travel to London.

The following is a partial list of cities serviced by courier companies:

- Amsterdam
- Bangkok
- Berlin
- Brussels
- Buenos Aires
- Cairo
- Chicago
- Dallas
- Dublin
- Frankfurt
- Geneva
- Hong Kong
- Houston
- London
- Montreal
- Nairobi
- New York
- Paris
- Rio de Janeiro
- Rome
- San Francisco
- Sao Paulo
- Seattle
- Singapore
- Seoul
- Sydney
- Taipei
- Tel Aviv

"I was a Courier Air Traveler"

Patrick S. Knaggs is a student who took this book's advice and traveled as an air courier to Europe during one of his summer breaks. Here is his story:

"First of all, I checked the local paper for a cheap way to New York. I found an ad in the classifieds that said, 'Drive my car to New York, I will pay for gas.' The guy gave me $200 for gas and expenses. I then posted a sign on the ride board at the local college and found someone to share the gas and driving to New York.

"The actual gas was only $100 [and the university student paid half of that] and I visited friends along the way and stayed with them for free. In New York, I stayed in a youth hostel for $10 a night and met lots of interesting people.

"I started calling the courier companies listed in the *Courier Air Travel Handbook* and got a flight that day to Oslo for $99 round trip. The company, Now Voyager, offered flights for $99 round trip to Oslo and Frankfurt. I flew on KLM Airlines and got frequent flyer mileage. I couriered one small package, but didn't have to do anything. I got free beer and a shrimp dinner—it doesn't get any better than this.

"A guy met me at the airport in Oslo and took the package (and I was still up fifty bucks since leaving Arizona). I spent time in Oslo, Copenhagen, and Amsterdam during my week in Europe. I picked up a return flight in Amsterdam back to New York and again stayed in the youth hostel.

"I called Auto Driveaway in New York and picked up a car in two days. I again shared the driving and expenses with a friend. I drove to San Francisco and visited more friends, then drove back to Phoenix.

"The whole trip cost me $300—and it was the best summer of my life. The *Courier Air Travel Handbook* was the best investment I have ever made."

Part 2

COURIER COMPANY DIRECTORY

T he following pages list present courier companies. Please note proper times to call; this will save you time and money. The phone numbers provided do change at times. At the time of printing, all numbers were current. Every attempt was made to locate toll-free numbers; however, these number are often closely guarded secrets.

It is expected that in the future there will be many additional cities from which courier travel will be originating, including: Boston, Denver, New Orleans, Phoenix, Detroit, Washington, D.C., and Atlanta.

Courier companies based outside the United States are listed beginning on page 50.

NEW YORK

Courier Company: ABLE TRAVEL & TOURS

Able Travel & Tours is a full-service travel agency. They can schedule courier travel from New York to London and Paris. Additionally, they can provide other discount travel to Western and Eastern Europe. They are one of the few places that specialize in Eastern Europe. If this peaks your interest, call Able Travel & Tours.

Phone Number: (212) 779-8530

Times to Call: 10:00am to 4:00pm, EST. Ask to speak with Ed. He is very helpful and quite knowledgeable about both courier and non-courier international travel.

Restrictions: Vary according to destination.

Prices: London or Paris for $295 ($350 during the summer).

NEW YORK

Courier Company: AIR FACILITIES

There are many flights to South America. Specifically, Air Facilities offers courier flights to:

- Caracas
- Santiago
- Rio de Janeiro
- Buenos Aires

Phone Number: (718) 712-0630

Times to Call: 11:00am to 5:00pm, EST.

Restrictions: Vary according to season.

Prices: $100 to $400 roundtrip.

Other comments: Air Facility also has offices in Buenos Aires, Rio de Janeiro, Santiago and Quito. See page 61 for phone numbers in these cities.

NEW YORK

Courier Company: AIRHITCH

Airhitch specializes in space-available travel and is designed for the extremely flexible traveler. They offer flights to every major city in Europe. Additional offices are located in Paris, Amsterdam, London, Munich and Milan. You can depart from:

- New York
- Newark
- Los Angeles
- San Francisco
- Seattle
- Ft. Lauderdale
- Miami
- Tampa
- Detroit

Phone Number: (212) 864-2000

Times to Call: 10:00am to 5:00pm, EST.

Restrictions: You must give them a five-day range, and three choices of destinations. You must accept the city offered or you forfeit your fare.

Prices: To Europe, prices are:
- $160 one way from East Coast
- $229 one way from Midwest
- $269 one way from West Coast

NEW YORK

Courier Company: COURIER NETWORK

Courier Network offers flights from New York to:

• Tel Aviv

Phone Number: (212) 691-9860

Times to Call: 7:00pm to 9:00pm, EST.

Restrictions: Flights are booked months in advance.

Prices: $400 to $500 RT.

NEW YORK

Courier Company: COURIER TRAVEL SERVICE

Courier Travel Service is a courier broker. They provide assistance and make reservations. They offer flights from New York to:

Amsterdam • Brussels • Copenhagen • Frankfurt • Hong Kong • London • Madrid • Milan • Paris • Rio de Janeiro • Rome • Singapore • Stockholm • Tel Aviv •

Phone Number:
- (800) 275-2359; (800) 922-2359;
- (516) 374-2299; (212) 836-1989
- Ask for Marvin.

Times to Call: 10:00am to 5:00pm, EST.

Restrictions: $100 return guarantee is required for some flights.

Prices: Most flights $249 round trip.
Prices lower for last-minute trips.
Sample 1992 prices:
- NY to London: $199 RT
- NY to Copenhagen: $199 RT
- NY to Madrid: $199 RT
- NY to Hawaii: $479 RT
- They also offer non-courier flights from New York to California for $298 RT.

NEW YORK

Courier Company: DISCOUNT TRAVEL
INTERNATIONAL

Discount Travel International is extremely helpful and offers courier flights to most major cities in both Europe and South America:

Athens • Amsterdam • Barcelona • Brussels • Caracas • Copenhagen • Dublin • Frankfurt • Hong Kong • London • Madrid • Milan • Oslo • Paris • Rio de Janeiro • Rome • Santiago • Stockholm • Zurich

Phone Number: (212) 655-5151; (212) 362-3636
(212) 362-8113

Times to Call: 10:00am to 5:00pm, EST.

Restrictions: Vary according to destination.

Prices: Most flights range from $100 to $300 RT. Great savings for last-minute flights. On one day in March 1992, they offered four flights for less than $100 each RT.

NEW YORK

Courier Company: EAST WEST EXPRESS
Phone Number: (516) 561-2360

East West Express previously had flights from New York to Hong Kong, Seoul and Sydney. They currently offer courier flights to:

- Manila

Courier Company: JUPITER AIR
Phone Number: (718) 656-6050

Jupiter offers flights from New York to :

- Hong Kong

The current price is $606 RT.

NEW YORK

Courier Company: HALBART EXPRESS

Halbart Express has one of the largest selections of courier destinations available. They send over 25 people daily to Europe as couriers, six days a week. From New York they fly to:

Athens • Amsterdam • Barcelona • Brussels • Copenhagen • Dublin • Frankfurt • London • Madrid • Milan • Oslo • Paris • Rome • Stockholm • Zurich

Phone Number: (718) 656-8189
(718) 656-8279

Times to Call: 10:00am to 3:00pm, EST.

Restrictions: Vary according to destination.

Prices: Vary according to season. Occasionally round-trip tickets are available for $100. Most flights are $199 RT–$299 RT depending on season.

up to 2 mos. ahead

NEW YORK

Courier Company: NOW VOYAGER

Now Voyager is a courier broker who provides assistance and makes reservations. It has one of the largest selections of courier flights in the world. In addition, there are opportunities for domestic travel at heavily discounted fares. From New York they fly to:

Amsterdam • Bangkok • Brussels • Copenhagen • Frankfurt • Hong Kong • London • Mexico City • Milan • Oslo • Paris • Rome • Singapore • Sydney

Phone Number: (212) 431-1616

Times to Call: 11:00am to 5:30pm EST, Monday through Friday. Call the number after 6:30pm first to listen to the recording.

Restrictions: $50 registration fee.

Prices: Tremendous discounts. Sample prices: NY to Mexico City, $75 RT; NY to London, $99 RT; NY to Frankfurt, $150 RT; Miami to London, $150 RT; Houston to London, $199 RT. Most flights to Europe cost $199 RT. They also offer discounted domestic tickets.

NEW YORK

Courier Company: RUSH COURIER

Good opportunity if you want to travel throughout the Carribean. There are many inexpensive flights from San Juan to other islands. From New York, Rush Courier flies to:

- San Juan, Puerto Rico

Phone Number: (718) 439-9043

Times to Call: 9:00pm to 5:00pm, EST.

Restrictions: Flights available Monday through Thursday and Saturday only. 21-day maximum stay. Can stay longer for slightly more money ($50 to $100).

Prices: $200 RT. $250 RT during Christmas season.

NEW YORK

Courier Company: WORLD COURIER

World Courier offers courier flights from New York to:

- London
- Paris
- Mexico City
- Milan
- Zurich

Phone Number: (800) 221-6600
(718) 978-9400; (718) 978-9552
(718) 978-9408 (Recording of current courier flights)

Times to Call: 9:00am to 12:00pm, EST only.

Restrictions: Vary according to season.

Prices: Prices range from $200-$400 RT. Recently offered flight to Mexico City for FREE. Call for more details.

HOUSTON

Courier Company: NOW VOYAGER

From Houston, they offer courier flights to:

• London

Phone Number: (212) 431-1616 (NY)

Price: • $285 RT/$300 with luggage

See New York section for more information on Now Voyager.

LOS ANGELES

Courier Company: AIRHITCH

Airhitch is designed for the extremely flexible traveler. Space-available travel to numerous European destinations. See New York section for more information.

Phone Number: (310) 458-1006

LOS ANGELES

Courier Company: IBC PACIFIC

IBC is one of the largest delivery companies in the world which offers courier travel. Additional cities are expected to be added soon. IBC currently travels from Los Angeles to:

- Tokyo
- Bangkok
- Sydney
- Hong Kong
- Singapore

Phone Number:
(310) 607-0125
(415) 697-5985 (recording of current courier flights)

Times to Call: 10:00am to 3:00pm, PST.

Restrictions: Deposit of $500 required. Payment can be made by cash, money order, travelers checks and credit cards.

Prices: Prices vary according to season. Prices as low as $250 round trip to most Asian cities. Daily flights to Miami for $85 one-way or $175 RT. Currently uses Northwest Airlines, which gives considerable frequent flier mileage to Asia (enough to earn you a free round trip domestic ticket after just one courier flight)!

LOS ANGELES

Courier Company: JUPITER AIR

Jupiter Air flies from Los Angeles to:

- Hong Kong
- Singapore

Phone Number: (310) 670-5123

Times to Call: 9:00am to 5:00pm, PST.

Restrictions: Can stay up to one month.

Prices: $546 to Singapore; $536 to Hong Kong.

Other Comments: Jupiter Air has overseas offices in Sydney, Hong Kong, London, Tokyo, Seoul, Singapore, and Taipei. See page 61 for phone numbers in these cities. There are many opportunities for courier flights originating in these cities.

LOS ANGELES

Courier Company: MIDNIGHT EXPRESS

Midnight Express is based in Los Angeles. On Saturdays they offer flights from Los Angeles to:

- London

Phone Number: (310) 672-1100

Times to Call: 9:00am to 10:00am, PST.

Restrictions: One-week to six-month length of stay. Usually booked months in advance. Payment can be made with credit cards. You must live in the Southern California area in order to take a courier flight with Midnight Express. They had a problem with a person who failed to show for a courier flight due to an unexpected delay in another city.

Prices: Prices vary according to season. Price ranges from $300 to $400 RT.

LOS ANGELES

Courier Company: POLO EXPRESS

Polo offers courier flights from Los Angeles to:

- Hong Kong
- Sydney
- Singapore
- Melbourne
- London

Phone Number: (310) 410-6822

Times to Call: 9:00am to 5:00pm, PST.

Restrictions: Vary according to season.

Prices: Asia for $200 to $350 RT. Australia for $300 to $600 RT. London for $199 RT.

Other Comments: Office in London (see overseas courier locations) with many flights to Africa and Asia. All flights are on United Airlines. There is a two week stay on flight to London, you are allowed to check one piece of luggage. The Los Angeles to London flight is one that I occasionally take.

LOS ANGELES

Courier Company: WAY TO GO TRAVEL CLUB

The Way To Go Travel Club is a travel agency which handles arrangements for numerous courier companies. They offer a variety of services for the budget-minded traveler including charter, stand-by, discount, and courier travel. From Los Angeles, there are courier flights to:

Bangkok • Hong Kong • Jakarta • Kuala Lumpur • London • Melbourne • Mexico City • Singapore • Saigon • Sydney

Phone Number: (213) 466-1166; (213) 466-1126

Times to Call: 9:00am to 5:00pm, PST.

Restrictions: Must join travel club for $75 per year which allows you to fly at extremely inexpensive rates. (The best $75 you will ever spend.)

Prices: There are great deals through this company. There are opportunities to fly for extremely low prices. Sometimes flights are FREE for people able and willing to fly on very short notice. Examples: LA to Singapore for $175 RT; LA to Mexico City for $50 RT.

LOS ANGELES

Courier Company: SOS INTERNATIONAL
COURIER

From Los Angeles, SOS offers flights to :

• Mexico City

Phone Number: (310) 649-6640

Prices: Current price to Mexico City is $150 RT.

Courier Company: WORLD TRAVEL & TOURS

From Los Angeles, World Travel & Tours offers courier flights to:

• Seoul

Phone Number: (213) 384-1000

Times to Call: 10:00am to 4:00pm, PST.

Restrictions: Flights are four times per week on United Airlines; one month stay.

Prices: Current price to Seoul is $413 RT.

SAN FRANCISCO

Courier Company: POLO EXPRESS

From San Francisco, there are courier flights to:

- Hong Kong
- Bangkok
- Singapore
- London

Phone Number: (415) 742-9613

Prices: Asia flights are $300-$400 RT.
London flights are $199 RT.
Flights are on United Airlines.

See Los Angeles for more information about Polo.

SAN FRANCISCO

Courier Company: WAY TO GO TRAVEL

From San Francisco, there are courier flights to:

- Bangkok
- London
- Singapore
- Hong Kong
- Mexico City

Phone Number: (415) 292-7801

Prices: Mexico City for $125 RT.
Asia flights are $300-$500 RT.
London for $299 RT.

See Los Angeles for more information about Way To Go Travel.

Courier Company: JUPITER AIR

From San Francisco, they offer courier flights to:

- Hong Kong
- Singapore
- Manila

Phone Number: (415) 872-0845; (415) 872-6506

Prices: • $400-$500 RT.

SAN FRANCISCO

Courier Company: TNT-SKYPAK

TNT-Skypak offers courier flights from San Francisco to:

- Hong Kong

Phone Number: (415) 692-9600

Times to Call: 10:00am to 4:00pm, PST. You will be connected to a recording; request an application.

Restrictions: $200 deposit. Two-week stay.

Prices: Flights cost $450 round trip.

SAN FRANCISCO

Courier Company: UTL TRAVEL

UTL Travel currently offers courier flights from San Francisco to:

- Singapore
- Hong Kong
- Manila

Phone Number: (415) 583-5074

Times to Call: 9:00am to 6:00pm, PST.

Restrictions: Recently eliminated annual registration fee. $100-$200 deposit required. Some flights allow you to take luggage (a rarity in the courier industry).

Prices: Fares range from $400-$500 RT.

CHICAGO

Courier Company: TNT-SKYPAK

Courier flights are sometimes offered to London but you must check for availability. From Chicago, TNT-Skypak offers courier flights to:

- Mexico City
- London

Phone Number: (708) 453-7300

Times to Call: 9:00am to 3:00pm, CST.

Restrictions: Flights depart Monday through Thursday; you may stay up to one year.

Prices: Price is $200 RT or $100 one-way.

MIAMI

Courier Company: A-1 INTERNATIONAL

From Miami A-1 International flies to:

- Caracas

Phone Number: (305) 594-1184

Times to Call: 9:00am to 5:30pm, EST.

Restrictions: You are allowed one carry-on and one piece of checked baggage. Up to three month stay.

Prices: Price is $306 RT.

Courier Company: COURIER TRAVEL SERVICE

Courier Travel is based in New York. From Miami they fly to:

- London   • Madrid
- Paris

Phone Number: (800) 922-2359; (516) 374-2299

Prices: Flights to Europe are $249 RT.

See New York for more information.

MIAMI

Courier Company: HALBART EXPRESS

Halbart Express is located in New York, but there are courier flights from Miami to:

- London
- Paris
- Frankfurt

Phone Number: (305) 593-0260

See New York for more information.

Courier Company: DISCOUNT TRAVEL
                     INTERNATIONAL

From Miami, they offer courier flights to:

- London
- Madrid
- Caracas
- Rio de Janeiro
- Mexico City
- Montevideo

Phone Number: (212) 655-5151 (NY)
                     (212) 362-8113 (NY)

See New York Section for more information.

MIAMI

Courier Company: LINE HAUL SERVICES

Line Haul Services has many flights to Central and South America. From Miami they fly to:

Buenos Aires • Caracas • Costa Rica • Guatemala • Lima • Panama • Quito • Rio de Janeiro • Santiago • Santo Domingo

Phone Number: (305) 477-0651

Times to Call: 9:00am to 5:30pm, EST.

Restrictions: Most stays are one month long.

Prices: Some flights for as low as $100 RT. Most flights $200-$250 RT.

Comments: Extremely busy office.

MIAMI

Courier Company: NOW VOYAGER

Now Voyager is a courier broker based in New York.

From Miami they offer courier flights to:

- Buenos Aires
- Madrid
- Santiago
- London
- Rio de Janeiro
- Caracas

Phone Number: (212) 431-1616 (NY Office)

Prices: Most flights are $199-$300 RT.

See New York section for more information.

Courier Company: IMS COURIER SERVICE

From Miami they offer courier flights to:

- Jamaica

Phone Number: (305) 771-7545

Price: $175 RT.

MIAMI

Courier Company: TRANS-AIR SYSTEMS

From Miami Trans-Air Systems offers courier flights to:

- Costa Rica
- Quito
- Guatemala

Phone Number: (305) 592-1771

Times to Call: 9:30am to 5:00pm, EST.

Restrictions: Need to make reservations 2 to 4 months in advance.

Prices: Miami to Guatemala is $190 RT. Flights leave Sunday through Friday and return Tuesday through Saturday. The roundtrip return flight is good for one-year. Miami to Costa Rica is $190 RT and departs on Sunday only. Miami to Quito is $180 RT. Up to a 21-day stay. Flights leave Sunday through Thursday and return Tuesday through Saturday.

CANADA

Courier Company: F.B. ON-BOARD
COURIER SERVICE

Phone Number: Toronto • (416) 675-1820
Montreal • (514) 633-0740
(call 2:00pm to 5:00pm)
Vancouver • (604) 278-1266

From Toronto: Flights offered to London, Paris and Hong Kong. Must be 18 years old and have a valid passport; otherwise, there are no problems for foreigners flying from Canada or from the U.S. To Europe the prices are Cdn $300 RT, Cdn $400 RT in summer.

From Montreal: Flights to London, Paris and Hong Kong. They answer the phone in French. London and Paris are Cdn $300 RT

From Vancouver: Flights to London, Paris and Hong Kong. Prices are Cdn $350 RT and Cdn $450 RT in summer to London and Paris. Hong Kong cost is Cdn $900 RT and Cdn $1,000 RT in summer.

CANADA

Courier Company: JET SERVICES

From Montreal, Jet Services fly to:

- Paris

Phone Number: (514) 331-7470

Times to Call: 11:00am to 1:00pm, EST.

Restrictions: Must call far in advance because it is a very popular route. Remember they answer in French; ask politely if they speak English.

Prices: Price is Cdn $300 RT to Paris.

LONDON

Courier Company: COURIER TRAVEL SERVICE

Phone Number: (081) 844-2626
                     71-351-0300

From London, Courier Travel Service offers courier flights to the following United States and Canadian cities:

- Chicago
- Dallas
- Los Angeles
- Miami
- New York
- San Francisco
- Toronto

Prices to the United States range from £150 to £250 RT.

They also offer courier flights to these cities:

Basel • Geneva • Harare • Hong Kong • Johannesburg • Lisbon • Nairobi • Paris • Rio de Janeiro • Sydney • Tokyo • Toronto • Vienna

Many good bargains on these flights. London to Vienna is £80 RT. London to Paris is £50 RT.

LONDON

Courier Company: POLO EXPRESS
Phone Number: (081) 759-5383

From London Polo offers courier flights to these North American cities:

- Boston
- Detroit
- Miami
- Montreal
- New York
- Newark, NJ
- Pittsburgh
- Seattle
- Washington, DC
- Chicago

Great fares from London to the United States. All above flights are from £135 RT.

They also offer courier flights to these cities:

Abu Dhabi • Athens • Bangkok • Barcelona • Cairo• Dubai • Gabarone • Hong Kong • Jersey • Johannesburg • Kuala Lumpur • Mauritius • Nairobi • Singapore • Sydney • Tel Aviv

Many bargains to be found here. London to Berlin £50 RT. London to Munich £50 RT. London to Amsterdam £39.

LONDON

Courier Company: SHADES INTERNATIONAL TRAVEL

Phone Number: (0274) 814-727

From London, Shades International Travel offers courier flights to these North American cities:

- Boston
- Detroit
- Miami
- Montreal
- New York
- Philadelphia
- Pittsburgh
- Seattle
- Washington, DC
- Toronto

Most flights are £180 round trip. There are two courier flights daily to New York.

They also offer courier flights to these cities:

Abu Dhabi • Athens • Bangkok • Barcelona • Cairo • Dubai • Gabarone • Hong Kong • Jersey • Johannesburg • Kuala Lumpur • Mauritius • Nairobi • Singapore • Sydney • Tel Aviv

London to Athens is £95 round trip. London to Bangkok is £305 round trip. Many good bargains to be found through this company. All flights are on British Airways.

LONDON

Courier Company: JUPITER AIR
Phone Number: (081) 751-3323
• They offer courier flights to Sydney and Los Angeles.

Courier Company: MSAS EXPRESS
Phone Number: 01-890-1355

Courier Company: NOMAD COURIER SERVICE
Phone Number: (081) 759-9277; (01) 570-9277
• They arrange courier flights for many companies in England. There are many courier flights to the U.S.

Courier Company: F.B. ON-BOARD COURIER
Phone Number: (0753) 680280
• Courier flights from London to Canada

Courier Company: WORLD SPEED EXPRESS
Phone Number: (081) 897-6162
• You must be able to travel on very short notice.

Courier Company: LINE HAUL
Phone Number: (081) 759-5969

PARIS

Courier Company: HALBART
Phone Number: 45.87.32.30

From Paris, Halbart has courier flights to New York. There are only two flights weekly and they go quickly. The price is F1500 (US$266).

Courier Company: JET SERVICES
Phone Number: (33)(14) 862-6222

They offer courier flights from Paris to New York.

SYDNEY

Courier Company: JUPITER
Phone Number: (61)(02) 317-2113; 317-2230
• From Sydney they offer courier flights to:

  • Hong Kong   • Singapore
  • London   • Tokyo
  • Auckland

See page 61 for additional Jupiter offices that offer courier flights.

Courier Company: COURIER TRAVEL SERVICE
Phone Number: (61)(02) 698-3753

Courier Company: INTERNATIONAL COURIER
              TRAVEL
Phone Number: (61)(02) 317-3193
• From Sydney they offer courier flights to London.

Courier Company: POLO EXPRESS
Phone Numbers: (02) 693-5866
• From Sydney they offer courier flights to Los Angeles and Auckland.

HONG KONG

Courier Company: COURIER TRAVEL SERVICE
Phone Number: (852)(03) 305-1413

From Hong Kong they offer courier flights to:

London • Sydney • New York • San Francisco • Singapore • Bangkok • Tokyo • Seoul • Taipei

Courier Company: GREAT BIRD COURIER
Phone Number: (852)(03) 332-1311

From Hong Kong they offer courier flights to Honolulu for free (one-way) and US $300 RT. They also have a daily flight to Tokyo for US $125 RT with a stopover in Taipei.

Courier Company: INTERNATIONAL COURIER
TRAVEL
Phone Number: (852)(03) 718-1332

HONG KONG

Courier Company: LINE HAUL EXPRESS
Phone Number: (852)(03) 735-2167; 735-2163

From Hong Kong, they offer courier flights to:

Bangkok • Frankfurt • London • Taipei • Tokyo •
Vancouver

Courier Company: POLO EXPRESS
Phone Number: (852)(03) 303-1286; 303-1287

From Hong Kong they offer courier flights to:

Tokyo • Los Angeles • Sydney • Singapore • Bangkok

Courier Company: JUPITER AIR
Phone Number: (852)(05) 735-1886; 735-1946

From Hong Kong, they offer courier flights to:

Bangkok • Los Angeles • New York • San Francisco •
Sydney • Tokyo

HONG KONG

Courier Company: JNE
Phone Number: (852)(03) 736-8678

From Hong Kong, they offer courier flights to:

- Bangkok

Courier Company: WHOLEPOINT LTD
Phone Number: (852)(03) 718-0333

The following is a list of **Jupiter Air offices** that also offer courier flights:

Singapore
(65)(011) 545-9113

Taipei
(886)(2) 551-2198

Seoul
(82)(02) 665-6024

Tokyo
(81)(03) 444-6771

The following is a list of **Air Facility offices** that also offer courier flights:

Buenos Aires
(54)(1) 3220-7720

Rio de Janeiro
(55)(021) 252-9597

Quito
(593)(2) 566-233

Santiago
(56)(2) 698-8125

Part 3

More About
Courier Travel

What is that old saying, "You do not get anything for free"? Well, in the case of courier travel, this is only partially true. While you do have the opportunity to save on a ticket to nearly every major city around the world, there is a "price" to pay.

But first let's look at the positive aspects.

1. **The Money You Save.** The money you save should more than compensate for any inconveniences that may arise. For those of you on a limited budget and who had planned on traveling light as it is, this is a "win-win" situation.

2. **No Advance Purchase Penalties.** When dealing with an airline directly, you often have to pay a hefty price for tickets not purchased seven, fourteen or even twenty-one days in advance—a long time for you "spur of the moment" types. As an air courier, you will not be penalized for making travel arrangements only a few days in advance. (In fact, this can be your leverage with the courier company. If the company needs to sell a ticket fast, you will probably be able to purchase the seat for very little or even free.)

3. **Courier Travel Is Fun.** You will be exposed to a whole new industry. When you meet another courier in the airport, you will have much to talk about—cities visited, courier companies used, etc. So when you meet that other courier in the airport, sit down, have a drink, and get to know your new friend.

The pros are easy to see, but what are the cons? The cons start out with the fact that you will not be allowed to bring luggage to be checked in (as the whole basis behind courier travel is that you give up your luggage space in return for a discounted ticket). However, this does not mean you must travel empty-handed. Most couriers are very creative people. (If they were not, they would be paying hundreds of dollars more for the same flight!) Use your creativity to get around this problem.

You will be allowed to bring on the plane one or two carry-on bags. The airlines usually do not bother you provided that you do not attempt to bring on a huge suitcase that you intend to fit under your seat. Take two full bags of clothing as carry-ons. This should be more than enough clothing to cover a week or two in a foreign city.

In the event you need more room, there is something else you can do. Though the airline will only allow two bags to be carried on, there is no restriction on the amount of clothing you can *wear* on the plane. I am very serious about this. If you need a heavy coat where you are going, wear it on the plane. Do the same for a heavy sweater, shirts, and so on.

You can always bring in your pocket a rolled-up nylon bag on the plane. Once on the plane, start shedding some of your clothing. The airline only restricts you on the number of bags that you can bring on the plane. If you board with two bags and deboard with three, consider yourself creative.

Another "con" is the small hassle before and after your flight. Air courier companies usually require you to be at the airport one to three hours before the plane departs, depending on destination. And after your flight you will need to hook up with the courier representative at the other end. Try not to let this small inconvenience sway you though. It's small in comparison to the savings involved. Some restrictions apply. For example, you will not be able to make advanced seat requests, special meal requests, date changes, transfers or refunds. And, all sales are final.

Making Reservations

Once you have decided on your destination, it is time to contact your courier company of choice. The courier company will help you locate a date that is available to them and acceptable to you. Some companies have different ways of collecting payment: some accept credit cards while others accept only money orders or certified checks. The important thing to remember is that money talks. Usually, the first person to pay for a flight gets it.

Traveling With A Companion

There are several ways in which you can travel with a companion. The first is to attempt to arrange same day courier travel for each of you. This is possible because some companies send numerous couriers each day. There are times when two couriers are needed for heavy shipments.

If you travel on different flights, then the first traveler may utilize the extra time by making arrangements for the hotel or hostel. The more common scenario is for one person to travel one day and the other to travel the very next day. Most courier companies purchase tickets for the same flights each and every day.

The other person has the option of purchasing a full-fare ticket on the same airline, but they may pay $250 to $700 more just to sit next to you as opposed to a little inconvenience. The choice is yours.

Another option is to fly to different cities and hook up later. For example, one could fly to London and the other Paris; ground and sea transportation between the two cities is very inexpensive.

The Day of the Flight

The day of the flight, you will meet an agent from the courier company at the ticket counter (or other predetermined spot). They will usually ask that you be at the airport a minimum of two hours prior to the flight. Usually, the process does not take long. The courier

representatives are very helpful—you are actually doing them a great favor. Without this favor they would
not be in business.

You will not be required to do any lifting, carrying,
lugging, dragging, etc. The agent will place the shipment directly into the hands of the airline and then give
you a manifest. Another agent will meet you at the end
destination and pick up the packages. You will show the
manifest to the Customs Officer upon completion of the
flight. There is no need to worry; Customs Officers see
many manifests each day and know what to expect.

The agent you meet prior to flight will give you a
printed copy of instructions, which includes your return
flight information and instructions. You will usually be
responsible to act as a return courier also.

Conclusion

Now you have the information you need to travel
inexpensively and enjoy many exciting destinations.
This is an opportunity most people only dream about,
but you have the knowledge to make your dreams
reality. So good luck and enjoy your travels! Send me a
post card from your courier destination detailing the
courier company, price of the flight, and departure and
arrival cities. I am always interested in my readers'
experiences and comments concerning courier travel. If
I include your information in the next edition, I will
acknowledge your contribution and send you a free
copy of the book.

Part 4

OTHER DISCOUNT OPTIONS AND INFORMATION

The following is a list of travel companies that could save you money on international and domestic travel.

Access International, Ltd.
(800) 825-3633

Air Brokers International Inc.
(800) 475-9041
• Specializes in round-the-world trips.

ANZ Travel
(800) 735-3861; (213) 379-2483
• Specializing in Australia & New Zealand.

Apex Travel, Inc.
(800) 666-0025
• Specializes in discount airfares to Asia.

British European Travel
(800) 747-1476
• Good fares to Europe.
• Very helpful company.

Express Discount Travel
(619) 283-6324
• Discounts up to 50%.

Euro-Asia, Inc.
(800) 525-3876
• Specializes in discount airfares to Asia and Europe.

Discount Travel International
(800) 334-9294
• Up to 60% discounts on all types of travel.
• $45 annual membership fee.

Encore Short Notice
(800) 638-8976

Europe Through the Back Door, Inc
109 4th Avenue N., Edmonds, WA 98020
(206) 771-8303
• Carries many travel books.
• Offers Eurail/Britrail passes, youth hostel guides and many other services needed for European travel.

Fellowship Travel International
(800) 446-7667
• Low cost international fares.
• Call between 9am-5pm EST.

International Student Exchange Flights
(602) 951-1700
• Specializing in low cost flights to most cities in Europe.
• Offers Eurail/Britrail passes, youth hostel guides and many other services needed for European travel.
• Organization that has helped students for 33 years.
• Call for their current catalog and prices.

Japan Budget Travel
(800) 722-0797

Just Travel!
(800) 262-JUST (5878)
• Specializing in discount airfares to Asia. Up to 30% off.
• Open 7 Days a week.

Last Minute Travel Club
(800) 527-8646 (East Coast only); (617) 267-9800

• Great fares from East Coast to Europe.
• Outstanding deals from East Coast to Mexico or Caribbean.

Maharaja Travel
(800) 223-6862
• Great fares to Europe & India.

Moment's Notice, Inc.
(212) 486-0500

Pan Express Travel, Inc.
(212) 719-9292

People's Air Tours
(312) 761-7500

Travel Avenue
(800) 333-3335; (212) 719-9292
• Heavily discounted airfares to Europe.
• Around-the-world airfares for as little as $1569.

Traveler's Advantage
(800) 548-1116
• Sells unfilled space on charter flights, cruises & tours.

Uni Travel
(800) 325-2222; (800) 325-2027; (314) 569-0900
• Discounted international & domestic airfares.

Virgin Atlantic Airways
(800) 862-8621
• Usually the most inexpensive airline to Europe.

Worldwide Discount Travel Club
(305) 534-2082

Departure Cities

All Courier flights leave from the cities listed. It is your responsibility to get to the departure city. If you happen to live in or near New York, Los Angeles, London, Miami, or San Francisco there are ample number of flights departing from those cities. For the rest of us who do not live in those cities, we need to find our way to one of the many departure cities. If you live anywhere near New York (by anywhere I mean east of the Mississippi) it is to your advantage to get to New York. Your best savings are from New York. If you live in the Western part of the United States, then Los Angeles or San Francisco should be your goal.

Southwest Airlines is one option. Their fàres are usually the cheapest in the United States. Call them at (800) 531-5601. Some of their fares are as follows:

Phoenix to Los Angeles $29 OW, $58 RT
Chicago to Los Angeles $162 OW, $314 RT
Houston to Los Angeles $149 OW, $298RT

America West is another good choice for inexpensive flights. Call them at (800) 247-5692. They offer flights to New York and Los Angeles from most of the United States.

American Express and Continental Airlines are offering college students, who have an American Express Card, four domestic roundtrip tickets for $129-$189 each. Call (800) The-Card for more infomation.

Auto Drive Away Companies

Another option is an Auto Drive Away Company. This is where you agree to transport a car for a company from one location to another. The main advantage to doing this is free transportation. You are only responsible for the gas and your expenses. It does not cost you anything else to do this. The company will provide you a free car. There are opportunities to drive expensive cars across all or part of America. If you have ever wanted to drive across the country in a Corvette, BMW, or Mercedes, this could be your chance.

They give you plently of time to get across country. An example is eight to nine days to drive from New York to Los Angeles. This would give you an opportunity to see many great sights. Drivers are always in demand. They can even arrange a return car after you return from your courier flight (remember that is why you bought this book in the first place).

This is a great opportunity to bring a couple of friends to a departure city for courier flights. Two or three people could pick up a car in one city and drop off the car in New York or Los Angeles, and subsequently catch a courier flight. It is possible to travel around the world for free or next to nothing. Some companies will arrange a return car after your courier flight. You can not do any better than this.

The following is a partial list of reputable auto drive away companies. Check your local yellow pages for a list of others.

Dependable Car Travel
(800) 826-1083
3 offices:
New York • Los Angeles • Miami

- Driver must put up $150 deposit. It is refunded upon delivery of car.
- Company pays first tank of gas.
- Driver must be over 19 years of age and have a valid driver's license.
- There is a three person limit in cars. This is dependent on the type of car.

Auto DriveAway Co.
85 offices nationwide
(800) 346-2277
New York (212) 967-2344
Los Angeles (213) 661-6100
Chicago (312) 939-3600
Miami (305) 931-8330

- Drivers must be 21 years of age and have a valid driver's license.
- Deposits range from $200 and up. It is refundable by any office.
- Foreign drivers are welcome. Must have passport.

- Call Bob Ashenbrenner in the Los Angeles office. He is extremely helpful, and will assist you in getting to or from Los Angeles. It is possible to arrange a return car after your flight.
- Drivers are always in demand.

All America Auto Transport
(800) 942-0001
2 offices:
Washington DC • Los Angeles

- Driver must put down a $100 deposit.
- Driver must be 18 years of age and have a valid driver's license.
- Driver must provide four references.

Freighter Travel

Freighter travel is slow and fairly inexpensive. This type of travel is gaining in popularity once again, however, you must be flexible with your travel plans. It was this type of travel which gave us the expression "Slow boat to China". The following are a couple of freighter companies:

Columbus Lines
(212) 432-1700
- Ships leave from both U.S. coasts destined for Australia and New Zealand.

Lykes Lines
(800) 535-1861
• Ships leave from the East Coast of the U.S. destined for Africa and the Mediterranean.

The following is a list of a number of the books or newsletters available on freighter travel:

Freighter World Cruises
180 S. Lake Avenue, Suite 335, Pasadena, CA 91101
(818) 449-3106
• $27 for one year subscription. Highly recommended.

TravLtips
163-07 Depot Rd., P.O. Box 188, Flushing, NY 11358
(800) 872-8584; (718) 939-2400
• $15 for one year subscription; $25 for two years.

Freighter Travel Club of America
3524 Harts Lake Road., Roy, WA 98580
• $18 for one year subscription; $28 for two years.

Pearl's Travel Trips
9903 Oaks Lane, Seminole, FL 34642
(813) 393-2919
• Travel agency that specializes in freighter travel.

If interested in river travel through Europe contact:

Floating Through Europe
271 Madison Avenue, New York, NY 10016
(212) 685-5600

Passports

If you do not have a valid U.S. passport, you will need to apply for it a couple of months prior to your trip. Foreigners must have a current passport from their country. A U.S. Passport is valid for 10 years. The current charge is $65. The fee is lower if you deal directly with one of the thirteen passport agencies listed on page 78.

It is possible to get your passport in one day; however, you must be able to show that you are leaving the country in less than 72 hours. This will be very difficult to do if you are traveling as a courier. For an additional charge you can have your passport in one week. Your best bet is to obtain your passport long before your date of departure. Do not wait until summer–the lines can be extremely long. If you are not located near a passport office, the main post office in your city will provide an application.

What you will need to obtain a passport

• Proof of U.S. citizenship. A birth certificate or certificate of naturalization of citizenship is your best bet. The birth certificate needs to be from the city or county from where you were born. A hospital copy will not suffice.

• Proof of Identity. You will need either a valid driver's license, government identification, or certificate of naturalization of citizenship.

• Two passport photographs. You will need two 2"
x 2" color or black and white photographs. The pictures
from the photo booths are NOT acceptable. Any photo
shop should be able to assist you.

You can obtain your passport quicker by going to
one of the thirteen Passport Agency Offices listed below:

Boston Passport Agency
John F. Kennedy Building, Room E 123
Boston, MA 02203

Chicago Passport Agency
Kluczynski Federal Building, Suite 380,
230 South Dearborn Street
Chicago, IL 60604

Honolulu Passport Agency
New Federal Building, Room C-106, 300 Ala Moana Blvd.
Honolulu, HI 96850

Houston Passport Agency
1 Allen Center, 500 Dallas Street
Houston, TX 77002

Los Angeles Passport Agency
11000 Wilshire Blvd., Room 13100
Los Angeles, CA 90024

Miami Passport Agency
Federal Office Bldg., 16th Floor, 51 S.W. First Avenue
Miami, FL 33130

New Orleans Passport Agency
12005 Postal Services Bldg., 701 Loyola Avenue
New Orleans, LA 70113

New York Passport Agency
Rockefeller Center, Room 270, 630 Fifth Avenue
New York, NY 10111

Philadelphia Passport Agency
Federal Building, Room 4426, 600 Arch Street
Philadelphia, PA 19106

San Francisco Passport Agency
525 Market Street, Suite 200
San Francisco, CA 94102

Seattle Passport Agency
Federal Building, Room 906, 915 Second Avenue
Seattle, WA 98174

Stamford Passport Agency
One Landmark Square, Broad and Atlantic Streets
Stamford, CT 06901

Washington Passport Agency
1425 K Street NW
Washington, DC 20524

Visas

A visa is an official approval for you to enter a country. Currently over half of all countries are requiring them. You need to consult the courier companies, airlines, consulates, or embassies about whether you will need a visa. In order to obtain one, you will have to write directly to the consulate or embassy. Some visas will cost money; while others will be free.

If you are interested in having someone else do the leg work for you or you are in a rush, there are a couple of companies that, for a fee, offer this service.

Express Visa Service
2150 Wisconsin Avenue, Suite 20, Washington, DC 20007
(202) 337-2442

Passport Plus
677 5th Avenue, 5th Floor, New York, NY 10022
(800) 367-1818; (212) 759-5540

Inexpensive Alternatives to Hotels

Youth Hostels are a wonderful way to avoid costly hotel bills and meet many interesting people. There are over 3,000 youth hostels in Europe, and over 1,000 in the United States. The average cost for a night is $3-$20 in Europe and $7-$30 in the United States. For more information contact:

American Youth Hostel
1017 K Street, N.W., Washington, DC 20001, (202) 783-6161

Canadian Hostelling Association
1600 James Naismith Drive., Suite 608, Gloucester, Ont. K1B 5N4

YHA England and Wales
14 Southampton Street, London WC2E 7HY, England, 044 836-8541

YMCA/YWCA is another option for the budget minded traveler. You can get more information concerning YMCA/YWCA in Europe and the United States from:

YMCA, 101 North Wacker Drive, Chicago, IL 60606, (312) 977-0031

YWCA, 726 Broadway, New York, NY 10003, (212) 614-2700

YWCA, Clarendon House, 52 Cornmarket Street, Oxford OX1 3EJ, England

Camping is a third option for lodging. Contact the following organization for more information on European or American camping:

National Campers and Hikers Association
4804 Transit Road, Bldg 2, Depew, NY 14043, (716) 668-6242

Servas is yet another option for lodging. Servas is an International organization that joins together hosts and travelers. There are members all over the world. As a traveler, you will stay for free in the home of a host. It is an opportunity for both of you to learn about each others culture. There is an application process, interview and screening. For an application contact:

U.S. Servas Committee, Inc.
11 John Street, New York, NY 10038, (212) 267-0252

The following is a partial list of some inexpensive places to sleep either in the departure cities for your courier flights or just when visiting these great cities.

LOS ANGELES

Colonial Inn Youth Hostel
421 Eighth Street, Huntington Beach, CA 92648, (714) 536-3315
• Centrally located near Disneyland and Beaches.

Los Angeles International Hostel
(310) 393-9913
• Overlooking the Pacific Ocean.

LONDON

Holland House Hostel
Holland Walk, Kensington, London W8, 071-937-0748
• £14 per night–fills quickly.

Oxford Street Hostel
14-18 Noel Street, London W1, 071-734-1618
• Located in heart of London.
• £15 per night.

Palace Court Hotel
12-14 Pembridge Square, Baywater W2, London, 071-727-4412
• £8.50 per night

Swiss House Hotel
171 Old Brompton Road, South Kensington, London SW5 0AN,
071-373-2769
• Close to most of London's main attractions.
• Winner of the *Best Value Bed & Breakfast Award*.

Westpoint Hotel
170 Sussex Gardens, Hyde Park, London W2 1P, 071-402-0281
• Quality hotel in central London for budget prices.

MIAMI

Greenbrier (Miami Beach International Youth Hostel)
3101 Indian Creek Drive, Miami Beach, FL 33140, (305) 531-0051
• $10 per night and is located 1 block from ocean.

Miami Beach International Travelers Hostel
236 9th Street, Miami Beach, FL 33139, (305) 534-0268
• Budget accomodations for the international traveller.

Sol Y Mar International Youth Hostel
2839 Vistamar Street, Ft. Lauderdale, FL, (305) 566-1023
• Great location.
• $11 per night.

NEW YORK

Allerton House
130 East 57th Street, New York, NY, (212) 753-8841
• Women only. $35 per night.

Manhattan Hostel (Kenmore Hotel)
145 E. 23rd Street, New York, NY 10010, (212) 979-8043

New York International AYH Hostel
891 Amsterdam Avenue (103rd Street), New York, NY 10025
(212) 932-2300
• The largest hostel in the United States (480 beds).
• $18.75 per night for members/$21.75 for non-members.
• Call 1 month in advance to make reservations during summer.

Penthouse Hostel (Carter Hotel)
250 W. 43rd Street, New York, NY 10036, (212) 391-4202

William Sloane House
356 W. 34th Street, New York, NY 10001, (212) 760-5856
• $29 single/$41 double.

SAN FRANCISCO

The Essex Hotel
684 Ellis Street, San Francisco, CA 94109
(800) 45-Essex (USA); (800) 44-Essex (CA)
• A great hotel in the heart of San Francisco for only $49 per night.

San Francisco International Hostel
(415) 771-7277
• Near Fisherman's Wharf.

San Francisco International Student Center
1188 Folsom Street, San Francisco, CA 94103
(415) 255-8800
• $12 per night.

International Tourist Offices

The following offices will help you with your trip. They will provide valuable information about their countries. This information includes maps, lodging, exchange rates, sights, and so on. Their services are free.

Australian Tourism Commission
459 Fifth Avenue, New York, NY 10017, (212) 687-6300

Austrian National Tourist Office
500 Fifth Avenue, Suite 2009, New York, NY 10110, (212) 944-6880

500 N. Michigan Avenue, Suite 544, Chicago, IL 60611, (312) 644-5556

4800 San Felipe Street, Suite 500, Houston, TX 77056 , (713) 850-9999

11601 Wilshire Blvd., Suite 2480, Los Angeles, CA 90025, (213) 477-3332

2 Bloor Street East, Suite 3330, Toronto, Ontario M4W 1A8 Canada, (416) 967-3381

1010 Quest rue Sherbrooke, Room 1410, Montreal, Quebec H3A 2R7 Canada, (514) 849-3709

736 Granville Street, Suite 1220, Vancouver, British Columbia V6Z 1J2 Canada, (604) 683-5808

Brazilian Tourism Office
551 Fifth Avenue, Room 421, New York, NY 10176, (212) 286-9600

British Tourist Authority
40 W. 57th Sreet., 3rd Floor, New York, NY 10019, (212) 581-4700

625 N. Michigan Avenue, Suite 1510, Chicago, IL 60611, (312) 787-0490

350 S. Figueroa Street, Suite 450, Los Angeles, CA 90071, (213) 628-3525

2580 Cumberland Parkway, Suite 470, Atlanta, GA 30339, (404) 432-9635

94 Cumberland Sreet, Toronto, Ontario M5R 3N3, Canada, (416) 925-6326

Danish Tourist Board
655 Third Avenue, New York, NY 10017, (212) 949-2333

P.O. Box 115, Station N, Toronto, Ontario M8V 3S4 Canada, (416) 823-9620

European Travel Commission
630 Fifth Avenue, Suite 610, New York, NY 10111,(212) 307-1200

French Government Tourist Office
610 Fifth Avenue, New York, NY 10020, (212) 757-1125

645 N. Michigan Avenue, Suite 630, Chicago, IL 60611, (312) 337-6301

2305 Cedar Springs Rd., Suite 205, Dallas, TX 75201, (214) 720-4010

9454 Wilshire Blvd., Suite 303, Beverly Hills, CA 92012, (213) 271-6665

1 Dundas Street West, Toronto, Ontario M5G 1V3, Canada, (416) 593-4723

1981 McGill College Avenue, Suite 490, Montreal, Quebec H3A 2W9, Canada, (514) 288-4264

German National Tourist Office
747 Third Avenue, New York, NY 10017,(212) 308-3300

444 S. Flower Sreet., Suite 2230, Los Angeles, CA 90071, (213) 688-7332

175 Bloor Street East, Suite 604, Toronto, Ontario M4W 3R8 Canada, (416) 968-1570

2 Fundy, Place Bonaventure, Montreal, Quebec H5A 1B8, Canada

Greek National Tourist Organization
645 Fifth Avenue, New York, NY 10022, (212) 421-5777

Hong Kong Tourist Association
548 Fifth Avenue, New York, NY 10036, (212) 869-5008

Irish Tourist Board
757 3rd Avenue, New York, NY 10017, (800) 223-6470, (212) 418-0800

Japan National Tourist Information
630 Fifth Avenue, New York, NY 10111, (212) 757-5640

165 University Avenue., Toronto, Ontario M5H 3B8 Canada
(416) 366-7140

Korea National Tourism Corporation
460 Park Avenue, New York, NY 10022, (212) 688-7543

Mexican Government Tourism Office
405 Park Avenue, Room 10022, New York, NY 10022, (212) 838-2949

Netherlands National Tourist Office
355 Lexington Avenue, 21st Floor, New York, NY 10017, (212) 370-7367

255 N. Michigan Avenue, Suite 326, Chicago, IL 60601, (312) 819-0300

90 New Montgomery Street, San Francisco, CA 94105, (415) 543-6772

25 Adelaide Street., Toronto, Ontario M5C 1Y2 Canada, (416) 363-1577

New Zealand Travel Commission
630 Fifth Ave., Suite 530, New York, NY 10111, (212) 586-0060

10960 Wilshire Blvd., Los Angeles, CA 90024, (310) 477-8241

Spanish National Tourist Office
665 Fifth Ave., New York, NY 10022, (212) 759-8822

845 N. Michigan Avenue, Chicago, IL 60611, (312) 642-1992

8383 Wilshire Blvd., Beverly Hills, CA 90211, (213) 658-7188

1221 Brikell Avenue, Suite 1850, Miami, FL 33131, (305) 358-1992

112 Bloor St. West, Toronto, Ontario M5S 1M8 Canada, (416) 961-3131

Swiss National Tourist Office
608 Fifth Ave., New York, NY 10020, (212) 757-5944

260 Stockton Street, San Francisco, CA 94108, (415) 362-2260

154 University Ave., Toronto, Ontario M5H 3Z4 Canada , (416) 971-9734

Useful Organizations

Elderhostel
80 Boylston Street, Suite 400, Boston, MA 02116, (617) 426-7788
• Study programs in the U.S. and Europe for people over 60.

Experiment in International Living
P.O. Box 676, Brattleboro, VT 05302, (800) 451 4465; (802) 257-7751

London Student Travel
52 Grosvenor Gardens, London WC1, England, (071) 730 34 02

STA Travel
Over 100 offices worldwide. (800) 777-0112 (US)

Travel Cuts (Canadian University Travel Services)
187 College Street, Toronto, Ont. M5T 1P7, Canada, (416) 979-2406

Volunteers for Peace
43 Tiffany Road, Belmont, VT 05730, (802) 259-2759
• Publish an annual international directory of workcamps.

CIEE

The Council on International Educational Exchange (CIEE) operates a network of retail travel offices across the country. They provide travel assistance to students, teachers and other budget-minded travelers. Services they offer include low-cost flights between the United States and Europe, Asia, the South Pacific, Africa, the Middle East, Latin America and the Caribbean; rail passes; a range of tours from bicycling through Europe to trekking in Nepal; language courses; and travel insurance, guidebooks and travel gear.

The following is a list of Council Travel offices:

CALIFORNIA

2511 Channing Way, Berkeley, CA 94704, (415) 848-8604

UCSD Price Center, Q-076, La Jolla, CA 92093, (619) 452-0630

1818 Palo Verde Avenue, Suite E, Long Beach, CA 90815
(213) 598-3338, (714) 527-7950

1093 Brocton Avenue, Los Angeles, CA 90024, (213) 208-3551

4429 Cass Street, San Diego, CA 92109, (619) 270-6401

312 Sutter Street, Suite 407, San Francisco, CA 94108, (415) 421-3473

919 Irving Street, Suite 102, San Francisco, CA 94122, (415) 566-6222

14515 Ventura Blvd., Suite 250, Sherman Oaks, CA 91403 (818) 905-5777

CONNECTICUT

Yale Co-op East,77 Broadway, New Haven, CT 06520, (203) 562-5335

DISTRICT OF COLUMBIA

1210 Potomac Street NW, Washington, DC 20007, (202) 337-6464

GEORGIA

12 Park Place South, Atlanta, GA 30303, (404) 577-1678

ILLINOIS

1153 North Dearborn Street, Chicago, IL 60616, (312) 951-0585

831 Foster Street, Evanston, IL 60201, (708) 475-5070

LOUISIANA

8141 Maple Street, New Orleans, LA 70118, (504) 866-1767

MASSACHUSETTS

79 South Pleasant Street (2nd Floor), Amherst, MA 01002, (413) 256-1261

729 Boylston Street, Suite 201, Boston, MA 02116, (617) 266-1926

1384 Massachusetts Avenue, Suite 206, Cambridge, MA 02138
(617) 497-1497

Stratton Student Center, MIT W20-024, 84 Massachusetts Avenue
Cambridge, MA 02139, (617) 225-2555

MINNESOTA

1501 University Avenue, SE, Room 300, Minneapolis, MN 55414
(612) 379-2323

NEW YORK

205 East 42nd Street, New York, NY 10017, (212) 661-1450

356 West 34th Street, New York, NY 10001, (212) 564-0142

35 West 8th Street, New York, NY 10011, (212) 254-2525

NORTH CAROLINA

703 Ninth Street, Suite B2, Durham, NC 27705, (919) 286-4664

OREGON

715 SW Morrison, Suite 600, Portland, OR 97205, (503) 228-1900

RHODE ISLAND

171 Angell Street, Suite 212, Providence, RI 02906, (401) 331-5810

TEXAS

1904 Guadalupe Street, Suite 6, Austin, TX 78705, (512) 472-4931

3300 West Mockingbird Lane, Suite 101, Dallas, TX 75235, (214) 350-6166

WASHINGTON

1314 Northeast 43rd Street, Suite 210, Seattle, WA 98105, (206) 632-2448

WISCONSIN

2615 North Hackett Avenue, Milwaukee, WI 53211, (414) 332-4740

List of Recommended Travel Books

These books usually can be found at your local bookstore, library, or a travel bookstore. If you are unable to locate any one of these books, you can order directly from the publisher.

The Bed & Breakfast Directory. This book provides details on over 1000 B & Bs in the United States and Canada. A handy book when traveling to North America. Order from the Publisher at (212) 850-6418.

The Best Pubs of Great Britain. One of my favorite books. Order from the publisher at (800) 243-0495.

Birnbaum's Guides. These books focus on the moderate price range. discounted

Cheap Sleeps/Cheap Eats in London. A great book if you are going to London. Order from the publisher at (800) 722-6657.

Cheap Sleeps/Cheap Eats in Paris. A great book if you are going to Paris. Order from the publisher at (800) 722-6657.

China Solo: A Guide to Independent Travel in China Ideal for courier travelers. Order from the publisher at (703) 522-9550.

Europe For Free. A great book with lots of fun things to do in Europe for FREE. Order from distributor at (901) 521-1406.

Europe for One: A Complete Guide for Solo Travelers Ideal book for courier travelers. Order from publisher at (212) 725-1818.

Europe: Where the Fun is. A guide to where the action is in Europe. Order from distributor at (901) 521-1406.

Fielding's Travel Guides. Plenty of information in these books, however, much of it is in the expensive range. Look for his Budget Europe guides.

Fodor's Travel Guides. The books are for individual cities, as well as for countries. This could be of more help if you are only planning on seeing one or two cities on your trip.

Ford's Freighter Travel Guide. Order from the publisher at (818) 701-7414.

Frommer's Guides. An excellent choice for budget-minded travelers.

Gault Millau Guides. Refreshing, critical, and honest remarks are the trademark for this series.

Going Places: The Guide to Travel Guides. A great book that lists and descibes thousands of travel guides. There are comprehensive reviews on all the popular guides as well as many that you never heard of. Order from the publisher at (617) 423-5803.

Guide to Greater London: Hotels, Pubs, and Restaurants. Order from the publisher at (212) 682-9280.

Hippocrene Books, Inc. They publish travel reference books, travel guides, maps, and foreign language dictionaries. Order from the publisher at (718) 454-2360.

The Insult Dictionary: How to Give 'Em Hell in Five Different Languages. For those times when you need to chew someone out in French, German, Italian, Spanish, and English. Order from the publisher at (800) 323-4900.

John Muir Publications. They publish a whole line of travel books. Call for catalog at (800) 888-7504.

Let's Go Travel Guides. An excellent choice for the budget traveler.

Lonely Planet Publications. They offer a large selection of travel books. Order from the publisher at (800) 229-0122.

The Lover's Dictionary: How to be Amorous in Five Delectable Languages. For those times when you need to say something romantic in French, German, Italian, Spanish, and English. Order from the publisher at (800) 323-4900.

Moon Handbooks. This series is for the adventurous. Public transportation is the primary mode of travel for the users of these books. Order these books direct from the publisher at (800) 345-5473.

Vagabonding in the USA: A Guide to Independent Travel. One of my personal favorites. This book is a must if you are traveling around the United States. Order from the publisher: Ed Buryn, P.O. Box 720, Nevada City, CA 95959. (US $12)

List of Travel Bookstores & Mail Order Companies

British Travel Bookshop
40 W. 57th Street, New York, NY 10019
(212) 765-0898

Book Passage
51 Tamal Vista Blvd., Corte Madera, CA 94925
(800) 321-9785; (415) 927-0960
• Travel bookstore and mail order company.

Complete Traveller
199 Madison Avenue, New York, NY 10016
(212) 685-9007
• Travel bookstore and mail order company.
• Send $2 for current catalog.

Easy Going
1400 Shattuck Avenue, Berkeley, CA 94109
(415) 843-3533

Forsyth Travel Library
9154 W. 57th Street, Shawnee Mission, KS 66201
(800) 367-7984; (816) 384-3440
• Travel bookstore and mail order company.
• Call for current catalog.

Globe Corner Bookstore
40 Brattle Street, Cambridge, MA 02138
(800) 358-6013; (617) 497-6277

Harvard Coop
1400 Massachusetts Avenue, Cambridge, MA 02138
(617) 499-2000

John Cole's Book Shop
780 Prospect Street, La Jolla, CA 92037
(619) 454-4766

Latitudes
4400 Ashford Dunwoody Road, Atlanta, GA 30326
(404) 394-2772

Latitudes
3801 Grand Avenue S., Minneapolis, MN 55409
(612) 823-3742

Let's Go Travel
Harvard University, Thayer B, Cambridge, MA 02138
(800) 5LETSGO; (617) 495-9649
• Travel accessory mail order company.

Le Travel Store
295 Horton Plaza, San Diego, CA 92101
(619) 544-0005

The Map Store
120 South Sixth Street, Minneapolis, MN 55402
(612) 339-4117

Michael Chessler Books
P.O. Box 2436, Evergreen, CO 80439
(800) 654-8502; (303) 670-0093
• Travel book mail order company.
• Call for catalog.

Nomadic Books
401 NE 45th Street, Seattle, WA 98105
(206) 634-3453
• Travel book mail order company.
• Specializing in budget travel books.

Open Air Books & Maps
25 Toronto Street, Toronto, Ont., Canada M5C 2R1
(416) 363-0719

Phileas Fogg's Books and Maps for the Traveler
87 Stanford Shopping Center, Palo Alto, CA 94304
(800) 533-3644 US; (800) 233-3644 CA; (415) 327-1754

Rand McNally Map Store
23 East Madison, Chicago, IL 60602
(312) 332-4627

Rand McNally Map Store
595 Market Street, San Francisco, CA 94105
(415) 777-3131

Tattered Cover Bookstore
2930 East Second Avenue, Denver, CO 80206
(303) 322-7727

Travel & Things
5940 College Avenue, Oakland, CA 94618
(415) 547-6560
• Travel agency and bookstore.

Travel Books Unlimited
4931 Cordell Avenue, Bethesda, MD 20814
(301) 951-8533
• Travel bookstore and mail order company.

The Travel Bookstore
1514 Hillhurst Avenue, Los Angeles, CA 90027
(213) 660-2101

Travel Bound Bookstore
815 S. Aiken Avenue, Pittsburgh, PA 15232
(412) 681-4100

Travel Collection
8235 Shoal Creek Blvd., Austin, TX 78758
(512) 454-7151

Travel Experience
111 South Bemiston Avenue, St. Louis, MO 63105
(314) 862-2222

The Travel Gallery
1007 Manhattan Avenue, Manhattan Beach, CA 90266
(213) 379-9199

Traveller's Bookstore
75 Rockefeller Plaza, New York, NY 10019
(212) 664-0995

Wide World of Maps
2626 West Indian School Road, Phoenix, AZ 85017
(602) 279-2323
• 3 locations in Phoenix area.

ORDER FORM

To order additional copies of *Courier Air Travel Handbook*, just fill out the form below or call (800) 345-0096 (Credit card orders only). This book will make an excellent gift for budget-minded travelers.

Send check or money order to:

Thunderbird Press
5930-10 W. Greenway Blvd.
Suite 112B
Glendale, Arizona 85306

Please send _____ copies @ $7.95.

Shipping and handling: $2.75 for the first book, .50 cents for each additional book. All orders are shipped First Class Mail.

Name _____

Address _____

City _____ State _____

Zip _____

TOTAL _____